REAPER

REAPER

Jill McDonough

Alice James Books

FARMINGTON, MAINE

10 9 8 7 6 5 4 3 2 1

Alice James Books are published by Alice James Poetry Cooperative, Inc., an affiliate of the University of Maine at Farmington.

Alice James Books
114 Prescott Street
Farmington, ME 04938
www.alicejamesbooks.org

Library of Congress Cataloging-in-Publication Data
Names: McDonough, Jill, author.
Title: Reaper / Jill McDonough.
Description: Farmington, ME : Alice James Books, [2017]
Identifiers: LCCN 2016046095 (print) | LCCN 2016054057 (ebook) | ISBN
    9781938584268 (softcover : acid-free paper) | ISBN 9781938584428 (eBook)
Subjects: | BISAC: POETRY / American / General.
Classification: LCC PS3613.C3885 A6 2017 (print) | LCC PS3613.C3885 (ebook) |
    DDC 811/.6--dc23
LC record available at https://lccn.loc.gov/2016046095

Alice James Books gratefully acknowledges support from individual donors, private foundations, the University of Maine at Farmington, the National Endowment for the Arts, and the Amazon Literary Partnership.

Cover photograph: "MQ-9 Reaper prepares for landing" - U.S. Air Force photo by Tech. Sgt. Chad Chisholm – Released – December 17, 2010.

Contents

The Rise and Fall of Robots   3

Governing Lethal Behavior in Autonomous Robots   4

Name Day   5

A Short Instruction of the Creation and Making of the World   6

Car Wash   7

Negative Obstacles   8

Afraid   9

Offices   10

World's First   11

Oak Ridge   12

I Tell My Mother What I Read about Sky Burial   13

The Landline   14

Arches National Park   15

All the Time   16

What You Worry About   17

How We Do   18

Ode to the Makers   20

Snow Drones   21

My Sister Wants to Buy My Dad a Drone for Father's Day   22

Milk Fish   23

Nature's Rugged Robots   24

So Pretty   25

This is. Like. The Best. Time.   26

Laika   27

War with Computers   28

Rocket Man Had It Coming   29

Twelve-Hour Shifts   30

Easy to Lie   31

BigDog   32
LOFTY VIEW   33
Heirloom   34
Law of Torment   35
Big Data Overlords   36
Reaper   37
I Dream We Try Gun   38
Try   39
Looking at Saints and Talking about Robots   40
John Clare's First Trip to London   41
Big Stink, Necessary Evil   42
Code Names   43
Mars   44
Bad Decisions   45
The Beautiful Woman   46
Devil Pod   47
My First Murderer   48
Calling Predator "I"   49
Armed   50
Still Death   51
Of a Piece   52
In the Next Chapter   53
Rat's Ass   54
The Money   55
Times Square   56
Imperial War Museum, Duxford   57
Brandon Bryant: MQ-1 Predator Sensor Operator   58
Stoning the Drone   59
Bin Laden's Burial and the Bureau of Investigative Journalism   60
It's Not the End of the World   61
New Year's Ghazal, after Ghalib   62
War Alphabet   63

ACKNOWLEDGMENTS

Academy of American Poets' Poem-a-Day: "Twelve-Hour Shifts"

Agni: "Snow Drones"

Barely South Review: "Heirloom"

Bellevue Literary Review: "I Tell My Mother What I Read about Sky Burial"

Breakwater Review: "Code Names," "Stoning the Drone," and "Rocket Man Had It Coming"

Common-place: "Law of Torment"

DMQ Review: "Easy to Lie"

Hobart: "The Beautiful Woman"

Let the Bucket Down: "My First Murderer"

Malahat Review: "Mars"

Mead: "Rat's Ass"

Memorious: "Arches National Park"

No: A Call & Response on Gun Violence in America: "Afraid"

NO INFINITE: "I Dream We Try Gun"

Off the Coast: "Laika"

PANK: "The Money" and "The Rise and Fall of Robots"

Poetry Northeast: "The Landline" and *"A Short Instruction of the Creation and Making of the World"*

The Rumpus: "Brandon Bryant: MQ-1 Predator Sensor Operator" and "War with Computers"

ROAR: "Ode to the Makers"

Soundings East: "Nature's Rugged Robots," "Milk Fish," and "New Year's Ghazal, after Ghalib"

Take Magazine: "Car Wash"

The Threepenny Review: "Looking at Saints and Talking about Robots" and "Reaper"

Topology: "Oak Ridge"

Tupelo Quarterly: "What You Worry About"

truthdig: "Still Death," "Big Stink, Necessary Evil"

Unsplendid: "Devil Pod" and "John Clare's First Trip to London"

Write on the DOT: "All the Time"

These poems were written with support from a Wallace Stegner Fellowship at Stanford University, the Dorothy and Lewis B. Cullman Center for Scholars and Writers, a Visiting Artist Residency at the American Academy in Rome, a Visiting Writer position at Westminster College, a Joseph P. Healey Research Grant from the University of Massachusetts Boston, and a Lannan Literary Fellowship. Thank you.

I want to thank Maggie, Wendy, Sumita, Josey, and Katie for being smart, generous readers. Thanks also to John Gertsen and everyone who cleaned around me at Drink after last call and lights up.

I want to thank Brandon Bryant and Matt Martin, who contacted me when I published poems quoting them. Both let me know I got something wrong, and I've corrected the poems from their previously published versions to reflect that.

REAPER

The Rise and Fall of Robots

For Tom Miller

I go to the park to see the robots rise. Their makers
take them there to test them out. Gas-powered,
barrel-chested horses, sort of. Sort of headless, sort of
not. An off-leash Rottweiler sees them, tucks his head
against my hip. A woman asks to pet them. One man asks
to film. *Don't put it on Facebook*, the engineers say.
Don't worry; I'm a fan. Like fans won't put it on Facebook.
You know he totally did. Software Perception, Control
Systems, Electrical, and Chief Engineers. The LS3's
named Norfolk. It's a Bigger Dog: it, the robot, Norfolk,
he. The engineers, mechanics try to talk to me. They say
his brain, say *those black strips make it so he can see*
the leader, sound like me saying my iPhone can't or can *talk*
to the sky. There's no shared language for this. I don't know
from LIDAR, don't know to be afraid. Bigger Dog in the wild's
a miracle. The mechanics try to walk like him, point toes
to hooves and lodge them in the snow. Bigger Dog
follows. Corridor. Follow the leader. Tight. Bigger Dog cuts
too hard and hits a tree. He cannot rise. But then he does!
Fails better. We watch him learn. We hesitate. We try
to think like him. He steps on a rock, lurches, catches
himself. *What was that?* one engineer asks. *Take that,*
Nature! another one says. We laugh. Reporting this makes me
sound anti-robot, anti-Man-making-anti-Nature jokes. I'm
not. I could watch him rise and fall all day, and almost do.
Offered conversation, lunch, I freeze and shake my head, don't
want to stall Progress. Horizoned on top of a hill, Norfolk rises
up a future. Beautiful, and odd. But the engineers all turn
to look at passing real dogs. Bigger Dog tucks his legs and skids
down thirty feet of ice and no one catches it on film.
When he stands up I'm proud enough to weep. A mechanic
smiles, scratches somebody's pup behind the ears. We're in
a park. They talk about lettuce on hot sandwiches: it is,
we agree, a mistake. They do this all day, all workweek.
They're used to all the wonder. All this future that they make.

3

is the book I can't put down, keep marking up,
love for its bibliography, equations, names to drop

with engineers about new robot dogs.
The author makes a good case. But. Come on.

We can't govern crap: our country, cars, remotes, my
printer, old iPhone. In fifteen years we've had five

coffee makers, four toasters, three Crock-Pots. *Set
It and Forget It* doesn't work for long. And yet.

On the other hand. Abu Ghraib, Bush-Cheney, My
Lai, Iran-Contra: we did that shit on purpose. We

over-drone. We shock and awe. *HELicopter Launched
FIRE-and-forget* missile, we say, unconvincingly. Watch.

See what we did there? Yes: *HELLFIRE.* Americans, distracted
by shine: new weapons, cool killer robot planes. Acting

as if we have the right. Maybe robots, their hollow core,
can spare all us from seeing what's in ours. Maybe our

robot overlord president could avoid executive overreach.
Because for us it's more embarrassing. In us it's not a glitch.

4

Name Day

Daybreak the Clorox-like stuff for cleaning
gravestones, *FOGBANK* the secret ingredient in nuclear
bombs: *The material is classified. Its composition
is classified. Its use in the weapon, the process itself.*

So we forgot how to make more *FOGBANK*: great name.
Too secret. *Big Stink* the *Superfortress* bomber
that followed and filmed the *Enola Gay. Superfortress,
Studebaker, Stratocaster, Chrome Dome*. Tyehimba and I

watch the news, put on big man TV ad voices, say
Now in Transvaginal Ultrasound! over and over like it's
Technicolor, Stereophonic, Now in Stereo. Combat
drones in video games have names like *Hornet, Hobgoblin*. Go

back, to the first real ones: the *Kettering Bug*,
the *Firebee*. Then *Quail, Cardinal, Jayhawk*.
They grow. They shift in meaning, intent.
Hunter, Raven, now *Predator, Reaper. Dominator*.

My drone's tougher than yours *times infinity* the namers
all say. My proxy, my avatar. *O my America*, my country's
day broken open to stained gravestones, banked fog. Followers,
hunters, we dominate. We watch us reap what we sow.

A Short Instruction of the Creation and Making of the World

Orbis Terrae Compendiosa Descriptio, 1637

Rumold Mercator's name is perfect for his map. Half
equator, half Mercury: how could he go wrong?
I love his sea monsters, pink and green, winged,
eared, eyes squinched shut in fury. They're still

beautiful, still thrashing their Florida-sized tails. Mercator's
notes tell us God got started with something like lava,
something *having no shape or form att all.* He tossed it around
like a glassmaker, glassmaker with *vehement breath.*

God made the oceans *commen* to us all. Oceans
speckled as pigskin, *Groentland* almost as big
as the red-flagged ships, sails billowing off toward
Anthropophagi, other parts unknown. *America*:

squashed, mostly vacant. *Canada* just somebody's small town.
But *Africa*'s outline is almost perfect, the hills and rivers
of *Senega, Gambra, Serra Liona* detailed, familiar, colored
in by hand. 1637, and they already know

what an Africa's for: *Fare well, and make thy proffyt.*

Car Wash

Josey and I get *girl*ed a lot. People like us, want to be
our friends. They say *Hi, girls* or *What'll it be,*
girls, when they'd never call dudes *boys*, call some
straight couple *kids*. But don't worry about it. It's fine.
We're girls at the Auto-Rite; diners; tollbooths;
The Drinking Fountain, our favorite secret bar.
You can tell a secret in a poem and it will stay a secret
forever. No one reads poems except for me and you.
The Drinking Fountain's by the car wash, for after
the thud and squeak of cozy suds, jolt of correlator,
conveyer belt nudging us like baggage. We're lugged
as groceries, not up to us anymore. The car wash
is sexy—tugged into now languid, now hurried slaps
of fresh blue sudsy rags, taken over, into the private half
light, a tunnel of suds. So there is kissing, sudden happiness,
still. I Google, learn *mitter curtain*, part of the *pre-soak arch*.
I knew I'd love the lingo, knew there was more than undercarriage,
hot wax, Tire Bright. Albert *ladies* us. But *Hi girls!* calls Gina
or Linda or Nancy when we walk in to the dim din, Brian Williams
on one TV, *Law and Order SVU* on the other. Josey gets a G&T
and a *Black Pearls* scratch ticket, or *Cash Blast*, spondees
that make me laugh. I get the beach of a five-count Bacardi
on ice with Coke, lime wedge in an eight-ounce glass. A white guy
tells Josey she looks like Michael Jackson. A black lady regular
rolls her eyes. The guy says *I'm not saying she looks like a man,*
and I shrug *But she does. Or, more than grown-man Michael, right?*
We all talk Michael's noses, Jackson Five to death, determine
when Josey's nose comes in. Gina tells us come back
St. Patrick's Day, her *conned beef* sandwiches, free
for everybody after three. If I have one more I'll cry, so in love
with the car wash, bar, with Josey, Boston, you. We go to the Drive-Thru
Car Wash whenever there's salt. Because our red Ford Ranger's
chassis rusted so you could see sunlight shine through. And the guys
at Morrison's Auto-Rite said, all sad, *You girls can't drive it anymore.*

Negative Obstacles

NPR has a story about robots asking *please*
don't pull that plug. People pull the plug but first
they cry. On YouTube I see the PETMAN robot,
his Superman thighs, poked with a ten-foot pole. His makers
shove him over, over and over again. I have no idea how
what they're doing, who they're making, works. Wondrous
as rainfall, as your own beating heart. MacGyver-y
young mechanics, engineers in sunglasses, one
Hello Kitty hat, run tests on Bigger Dog. Engine off,
his legs lose their will, collapse like he's a corpse. Watching
the robots stumble, rise, makes me proud to be
American. Or something: proud to live some place some
time where this is how we do. Proud of these new
creatures. And their people, making real-life C-3POs, robot
cats and mules and dogs. How they let us see ourselves
watching anything sort of die. Or struggle, rise again.
In *Governing Lethal Behavior in Autonomous Robots*, which
is almost as good as it sounds, the author suggests
we can't be trusted, but robots probably could.
We could program them to always be good guys.
No more bad kills, collateral damage. No more My Lai;
no hungry, tired, scared GIs; no more kids killed by drones.
We've seen too much *Terminator*, go straight to an Age
of Robots, robot overlords. But I, for one, welcome
discussion, distrust of human heads. The makers,
young men and women in Carhartts, in the woods outside
the lab, urge Bigger Dog past birches, oaks, over
lacily-lichened boulders, through a miracle of leaves. They lead
him to a *negative obstacle*, an edge, some new thing deep
he can't escape. They shove the joystick forward. And Bigger Dog
stops, stands stock-still. Not stubborn, not dignified or
sure. He doesn't look back, doesn't move. Just won't go any more.

Afraid

I'm not afraid of murderers, apparently, or walking alone at night,
what I'm supposed to fear. Forty, American, white,

employed: I've already won. But a quick ratty shadow in the street,
gunshots breaking air open, doubting what's under my feet . . .

Rachel says *you're afraid of everything* and I flinch because she's right.
Heights, rats, gunfire. I'm not afraid of getting shot,

the noise just makes me want to cry. Heights:
not a roof, a bridge, a plane, but ice, ice

skating, ladders, any jolted precarious perch. I remember the shim
shaped rock I nicknamed "Lucky" the summer I painted houses, gripped

aluminum ladders that telegraphed trembling, ten
bucks an hour. The cheerful song I sang under my breath,

dipping and reaching, keeping everybody safe, ended
he's our Lucky rock his name is Lucky. Then I'd sing it over again.

Offices

The day I fell down I showed students the new
Sappho, drafts I got from the translator through Twitter,
talked about ways to love more the world. We worked
on the first line: How could anyone not always
be wanting more? Everyone wanting,
always wanting more. Everyone wanting *wanting*,
wanting to want more. Take it for granted: you want
a snootful of desire. Not holding hands and watching TV.
Not Yahtzee, Crock-Pot full of chili, beans. Not hearing,
after you puke with old-lady vertigo and apologize:
It was an honor. You get used to it, people falling down.
Instead think like saints would, before we knew from
inner ear. Imagine being tossed and wrecked
by a god in your bed, thrashed around like that
while thinking your soul was at stake. Wrestling
with god, or an angel. Jacob knocked his poor hip
out of joint. Or the angel did. We're lucky;
the doctors tell us *not a big deal, we'll keep an eye
on it, come back in a year.* One of these days
the news won't be good. Then we'll be dead.
For now, though, read *The New Yorker*, delete spam
next to me. I'm always wanting more of you, even
in the doctor's office, the Breast Center waiting room.
I always want your neck within reach of my mouth.
More of your pulse, more smell of your hair. Let's spend
more hours in offices, wanting to hedge more bets.

World's First

For Sara Lippincott, and for Kathleen Flenniken

Day and night shifts of schoolgirls in school yards, sumo
halls, pasting sheet after sheet of *washi*. Laughing
at rumors of *fusen bakudan*: balloons to lift and carry
bombs across the ocean. Who could believe it? The world's
first Intercontinental Ballistic Missile was made
of paper, children's paste. Soft, ambitious, loaded
with ballast, bombs, it rose *in the blue sky like a daytime star.*
They sent ten thousand off blind and made it
to Echo, Oregon and American Falls. To Walla Walla.
To Kadoka, South Dakota. Rising so high, pilots
confused them with Venus. One broke power lines near Hanford,
Washington, where we made what we needed for the world's
first A-bombs at the Hanford Atomic Reservation,
the world's first plutonium plant. It shut the reactor
down but not for long; we still filled Fat Man for Nagasaki,
still tested The Gadget. In Hanford, Washington,
we made plutonium all through the Cold War. River water
cooling reactors, returning to the river *as far as Pacific*
oyster beds along the Washington and Oregon coasts.
Hanford had a code name for radiation: *Shine.*
Shine on the wind in the air of Oregon. Idaho. Montana,
milk cows grazing there. One mother, conceived in the years
her mother worked at Hanford, told researchers *I understand*
that it could take years for you to know if anything is wrong.
I don't think anyone really knows if Hanford's radiation
will affect future generations. But I can't help but worry.

Oak Ridge

So when Roosevelt reiterated, "Can you hide $2 billion for a secret project that we hope will end the war?" Senator McKellar deftly replied, "Well, Mr. President, of course I can. And where in Tennessee do you want me to hide it?"

— Denise Kiernan, *The Girls of Atomic City*

It was good work, good
money. No one knew anything
for sure. Do what you're told
and don't ask why. Shut up
and color. Stick to your knitting.
A new kind of patriotism. *You wanted
your R high. That was better than Q.
Something was vaporized. There
was a Z. The E box caught
everything. Open the shutters. Maximize
the beam.* They made uranium-235,
called it The Product, shipped it
across the country in briefcases
handcuffed to men who'd get
a massage, a bath, a steak
when they arrived. *Pipes came in
and pipes went out.* They all saw
glints and flashes. Soldiers
were told to lie down
on their stomachs, faces
away from the blast.

I Tell My Mother What I Read about Sky Burial

When my mother tells me she wants her ashes scattered
in the water around Monhegan, I look at my sisters.

Didn't she tell us she wants to be scattered
on the Red Ribbon Trail? I ask them. They nod. *Mom,*

you can tell us whatever you want, but we're not
doing any of it. I just read this book about Tibet.

We're giving you a sky burial. When she asks
what's that I tell her in Tibet they take the body,

dismember it, chuck the limbs in the air and birds
of prey come grab it bit by bit. It's true. I make

the breaking sounds, pretend to twist her limbs off
at the hinges like I'm cracking open a chicken carcass,

chuck them in the air to birds. Pop, chuck. Pop, chuck.
I don't like that, she says. *What, this?* I say, *Pop, chuck?*

That's what they do in Tibet? she says. *No wonder*
the Chinese don't like them. I'm glad they're not free.

The Landline

We let go of the landline, lose
the numbers that told us who we were, once, how
we get home. 522-0092
Josey's number, then mine, ours, before
you needed area codes. *Back in the day.*
Get off my lawn. 250 E. 57th,
I recited, grim about New York City cabs,
staying safe in some vast unknown. Now
I guess I'd say the corner: 57th and 2nd,
but I'd never go there. It's gone now, that time,
apartment, its carpet and popcorn ceiling, orange couch.
I don't know the boy I used to meet there,
and his mother doesn't live there anymore. 86104
was someone's PIN number once, not mine.
PIN number. ATM machine. Whose?
I'll never tell. We sang it, hot and close,
a half dozen of us, half in love
with each other, our marvelous lives, singing
86104 so it made the Fugazi
song "Waiting Room," that pause still filling my nose
and eyes with some chemical trace of reckless
pleasure, sunrise, smoke. I have forgotten
my college P.O. Box number, Hill Street Middle
School, Asheville Junior High and High School
locker combinations, the numbers and words
on the note I wrote, brought home first grade. *1. Yes.*
2. Kleenex. 3. Noon. Proud I'd remembered what
my mother asked, written Miss Grapel's answers
on the lined paper we used—the soft gray pulp
that tore when you bore down or tried erasing,
lined in alternating solid and broken
lines, all Carolina blue. I thought my mother
was 34 for years—how, how could she age?

Arches National Park

Driving south to Arches the churches
change from Latter Day Saints to Fountain of Faith
to Fifth Assembly, and the landscape's littered
with forgotten handiwork, clay a waste
of breath. Huge, clumsy bones and arches:
Delicate Arch, a giant failed rib. Fin
Canyon, Eye of the Whale. A prototype, the first
try. Garden of Eden, Balanced Rock—here
He's just messing around, a Child
of Architects, leaving out His blocks.
Nearby, rock faces are scratched with symbols
drawn by early Us: men, bear claws, scrub
jays, deer. Circles inside circles, symbols
we forgot. What they didn't draw: these
arches. They took them for granted,
couldn't see the things I can't stop looking at.
We are happy in the sunlight, want to catch
this light on these red rocks. So all of us
hold our shining iPhones up before
us. We use what we take for granted, beam
images of what we love up to the sky.

All the Time

Students translate Sappho's speechlessness
with *broken tongue*, or *I can't get
the words out*. One writes *I want
to tell you a million and one things* and I
am happy, think of one, one of the million and one
things I love about marriage. Or
at least being married in mine. Wanting
to tell her something, knowing
I don't have to tell her now. Slipping down
under into sleep, say. Or just losing the frayed
and fragile hem of it, too distracted
to remember what I need her to know.

The students already know how,
starstruck, lovejammed, we don't know
what to say. All you want to do is find
the right thing, say that which will keep the beloved
close by. But they don't know yet that once
you pull off the trick and make her love you back,
you have all the time in the world to think
of it. The new right thing, or whatever else it was
you wanted to tell her: you bought a rug, say. Picked up
her dry cleaning. Remembered what made her laugh
in Spain, remembered touching her chin
with your thumb. Car rides and movie lines, waiting
in windowless offices to hear something else is benign.
All the up-early-with-jet-lag, all the wait-at-the-bar-
to-be-seated, all the folding of shirts now freshly charged
with this: we have all the time anybody else
in the world gets. All the time we need to say
the right thing, find new right things to say.

What You Worry About

For Susan

I worry about my teeth, and bleeding
on your white sheets. You worry
about ugly blancmange, what
we're going to eat. *I worry
about the position of the dog's
stuffed animals. I like the arm
of the monkey to be over
the octopus to show that they
are comrades.* I look at you like
you're crazy, and I'm a patient
kind of doctor. Kind.
You sigh and say, *I know.*
I worry about money, usually. Where
the next money comes from and
how soon. When I have some
money I am cracked open, calm,
breathe deep. Worry-free. Ready
for anything. You worry
about constructing a lamb cake, whether
it can stand upright or have to be
a *bas-relief.* If *Cornus mas* would ever
bloom in a zone 5. *I worry about walking
between parked cars.* While
you're sleeping? While you're falling
asleep? *Yes. Getting my legs
cut off.* I worry about that when I'm
walking between them, but not
when I'm safe in my bed. I praise
you for always walking over subway
grates, when I skirt them, walk around.
That's not my issue, you say, while
I skirt one, walk around.

How We Do

We haven't yet found artifacts from an alien civilization in orbit around the earth, or on nearby planets and moons, but we are creating them.
—Trevor Paglen, *Last Pictures*

He's talking about what happens, what could happen
five billion years from now. *An Age of Giant Squid*: wide-eyed
romantics floating, gazing up at the twinkling space

trash we'll leave behind. In the future will there be eyes?
Probably, he grants. Granted a future near stars.
In the shorter long term we're eating

garbage, living in vintage tents. Some of us on
the vanguard, now, some of us already there.
In the future we don't value children, children's

lives. The future starting now, then, any point in the Age
of Us. The snow blows in sideways, the potholes fill
with slush. In the future there are no potholes!

Because no pavement plus which *Giant Squid*.
Because devastating holocaust, sure, but that's just
jumping the gun. The gun: at some point time's

up for us. At some point we'll all be extinct.
In the long afterward, there will be time for another
Age of Dinosaurs. An *Age of Crows* or Cows.

In the long afterward there will be no one to know
whether you loved your children, or theirs, or any
body's child. The EchoStar XVI will broadcast fifteen

years, then ditch to *"graveyard orbit," power down and die.*
But the pictures will stick, pictures Paglen picked. Cloned
cows, the view from a Reaper. The bees we teach to taste bombs.

Walleyed kids with fucked-up heads, our fault. No mother
and child, no baby Jesus. Not even a Christ on the cross,
the picture we keep, use now, to remind us how we do.

Ode to the Makers

For Nadia Cheng

When you take the future out for drinks she ends
up paying. The future looking good on paper,
the future looking good. 3D printing
organs for infants; valves for *a cartoon blob*
of flubber, the *Squishbot* DARPA wants. DARPA
sounds like Darth Vader, Dark Arts, but it's *Defense*
Advanced Research Projects Agency. We shop
for what we want from the smartest people we have.
When the DARPA guy shows up the first time, talks
to grad students at MIT, he says
he *just* wants *something you can pour through a hole*
and then it comes out crawling. Nadia explains
how: *elephant trunk* not *WALL-E.* Her robot's
soft sections, valves and levers. Prototypes:
condoms filled with ground coffee, *actual mechanical*
valves she says, displaying disdain for what
we cannot touch. We talk *The Walking Dead*,
drink Corpse Revivers, eat a shitload of fries.
I ask what she calls her SquishBot, she tells me she calls
it her *baby.* I love using condoms to make
this baby, new being. The opposite of the body,
body: the first 3D printer, I try, delighted,
a little drunk. The future nods, indulgent.
My robot won't kill anybody, she says of the SquishBot.
Later, I'll watch its first movements, uncanny rise and fall
sudden, then fluid. Uncharted dangle, deliberate
lift and turn, wondrous as a brand new baby boy's.

Snow Drones

We go see the Rockettes start up with jingle bells, light-up
antlers, brown velvet leggings on thirty-six dancing girls,
pulling Santa's sleigh. This is America, privilege, wonder:
I love it. The Rockettes a kaleidoscope, satisfying geometry.
Their synced legs sexy, sure, but also *organized*. Watching
them, we're soothed, made whole. Dancing girls in coats
on a double-decker bus. In Santa suits. In loops
of partridges, pear trees, five golden rings. In red or green
sequins. Wrapped like gifts, like Starlight Peppermints. Glinting
with crystals and lights. Rosy-cheeked, unsmiling women
dressed as toy soldiers, facing a prop cannon that goes *BOOM!*
So they slump back, lock arms and fall too slowly, in a unison
that makes me wince. They break time open, make all
the sparkles and kicking stop too long, a second too long,
let in real soldiers, cannons we don't pay to think about.
Before the Living Nativity's robes and camels, before
Unto You A Child Is Born, snowflakes rise out
of the orchestra pit. They dip and bob and we understand
what we're seeing, say, at once, delighted, *Drones!* We tilt
our heads back to watch them glide, miraculous,
ignoring the gleaming half-dressed women dancing
their legs off for us. We gawp at the drones, the absurd snow
drones, whisper *they see you when you're sleeping* and laugh.
Then the ticker-tape snow starts falling on us, on the audience,
keeps falling. Thick and ridiculous; wealth of it, a blinding
plenty. It fills our clothes and purses, becomes something we
shuffle through to get out. For days we find it in our hair,
our pockets. It's everywhere; we can't shake it. All for us.

My Sister Wants to Buy My Dad a Drone for Father's Day

But I'm old fashioned, a stick
in the mud, thinking of Ravens,
Predators, Reapers. What a pain
in the ass to have a sister like me,
who won't just fork over her share
of the dough. Who has to *feel* dumb
ways about things, distracted by names
like DarkStar, ScanEagle, Shadow,
WaspBlock. Who doesn't want a toy
airplane with a camera? My dad is not going
to shoot suspected insurgents, hover
over his neighbors' homes for days.
Technology is fungible. Also
really cool. Drones don't kill people,
people et cetera. People drown
in water. But I still want to drink it.

Milk Fish

For livingunderdrones.org

Surveillance balloons over
Afghanistan, even cheaper
than drones. Chubby, white,
fishy with fins. In Helmand
they call them *milk fish*.
In Kandahar they're *frogs*
because big eyes. They get
shot at, still stay up. Raven,
the Switchblade, the Predator
drone. The Switchblade's
a kamikaze, will go down
where you tell it to bomb.
The Puma, the Wasp, Scan
Eagle, Global Hawk. The Raven
can crash-land and break
apart, get pieced back
together. You can't get them
down, can't make them go
away. *You have no privacy
anyway. Get over it.* They're
getting smaller, evolving down:
robobee, octoroach, nanoquad,
squishbot. *I can't sleep at night
because when the drones
are there I hear them
making that sound, that
noise. The drones
are all over my brain.*

Nature's Rugged Robots

"Scientists train honeybees to detect explosives"
—YouTube video, LosAlamosNationalLab

Bees like sniffer dogs, a swarm, robots
like bees. Harvard's robobee blog admires
elegance in flight, how real bees zip
from flower to flower, hover *stably with heavy*
payloads. God *wants* us to make robots, shows us
how with bees, snakes, rats. We take
permission, dominion, make honeybees
our robots, make drones that look like ravens,
littler ones like hummingbirds. We're fooling
each other, and sometimes the birds. The CIA's
Insectothopter looks like a dragonfly, sounds
like *thop thop thop*. A flock of pigeons at some border,
pigeon-colored camera strapped to one's chest. When?
Where? *Details of pigeon missions are still classified*. Oh,
DARPA, Los Alamos. Real and the robot; birds
and bees with eager, trusting, sugar-loving tongues.

So Pretty

So pretty we say to strangers sharing
a cab over a causeway, or
next to us, en route to JFK. Shaking

our heads together over our oval of sunset,
our lightning lighting up our clouds. 6A's
reading up on what happens after death,

the spirit-world powers she'll get when she's divine.
Strangers are crazy. But we can still agree:
so pretty, the child's hair in the Stop & Shop line,

somebody's laughing baby on the T. Her
little body! Your neighbor's fresh
clapboards, freshly-caulked seams. Fragrant lure

of stripes of fresh-mown grass. *So pretty*: so
empty, so touching, how we fall so short so close.

This is. Like. The Best. Time.

For Max Lobovsky

I'm embarrassed I can't think of anything
I want 3D printed. Suddenly able
to make anything I can imagine, I think
of the broken dial on the blender, the earring I lost
last year. Pathetic as those guys who make
AR-15s with 3D printers: little
boys playing guns with sticks. Humans: you
can count on us to always miss the point.
In college I asked my smartest friend what she'd do
if sentenced to life in prison. I figured we'd all
agree death row's a good idea. Because
wouldn't you rather just *die*? But she said she guessed
she'd study law, become a lawyer. Help
the other inmates, you know. I'm still embarrassed.
When I tell Max-the-3D-printer-guy
I wrote about BigDog, LS3, robots
I love, he says *Was it like a horror dystopian
future poem?* Nah. Too easy. Fish
in a barrel, with 3D-printed guns. Max makes
3D printers, gives them each a name
instead of a serial number. Out there, now,
new to the world, the makers own these fresh wonders:
Glib Lapwing, *Necessary Ant*, or *Chubby Dog*.

Laika

The U-2: our spy plane, before drones. So,
piloted by pilots, who sometimes got
shot down. Gary Powers remembered the falling
fondly: *just falling perfectly free*, and then
the parachute, *better than floating
in a swimming pool.* He passed fields
and forests, *everything cold, quiet,
serene. A large section of the aircraft
floated by, twisting and fluttering
like a leaf.* But he landed, skipped
the cyanide some of us thought he should
take. The Russians picked him up, gave
him a Laika brand smoke. *How like an American
cigarette it was.* The packet—you can still
find them online—is beautiful, half lapis
sky, gold stars. Little sickle
of moon. Sputnik streaking by. And Laika:
once a Moscow stray, first dog in space. First
anything to orbit earth. First one to die
up there. Her doggy face is nobly portrayed.
She died in hours: too hot, no air. But her corpse
circled the earth two thousand, five hundred
seventy times before she crashed and burned.
Chin up, she looks past you, into her airless space.

War with Computers

We don't make war with computers.
—Captain Kirk in *Star Trek*, "A Taste of Armageddon," 1967

We hover at five thousand feet. It's not a fair
fight, but neither are IEDs. We watch day and night.
We don't make war with computers, though; we're not there

yet, are we? When did we sign up for this? Where?
We sing *God Bless America, through the night with a light
from above,* hover at five thousand feet. It hardly seems fair

to the operators, the pilots: twelve hours in the chair,
home for breakfast, bed, then back to someone else's sunrise.
We don't make war with computers. We're not there

to see the strikes wipe humans out: sudden glare
on the screen, infrared blooming white and wide.
We hover at five thousand feet. It may not be fair,

but it's hard to resist: bin Laden, bin Laden's lair,
got made by our unmanned planes, in the mini fun-size.
It's blood-cheap, war with computers: we're not there.

Not really here, either. All of us always everywhere:
work, home, faces lit by our phones. Killer apps fill the time.
We hover at five thousand feet. Apparently all's fair
in our wars, say our computers. We do what we want over there.

Rocket Man Had It Coming

After Lt. Col. Matt J. Martin, *Predator: The Remote-Control
Air War over Iraq and Afghanistan: A Pilot's Story*

The Rocket Man had it coming. The old man did not.
We train our lasers on one guy, another guy gets got.
I was unable to determine whether or not he got up,

I said, knowing if I didn't see him move, the old guy's shot.
Nobody means for it to, but sometimes shit
happens: one guy has it coming, another does not.

We hover and hover. We wait while we watch.
We look and we analyze and then take the shot.
I was unable to determine whether or not he got up.

Civilians think it doesn't matter, like the robot
erases guilt, our shitty mistakes. Nope: we're stuck
knowing Rocket Man had it coming, but the old man did not.

I'm not clear on what we're trying to do there, what
our job is, how what we do here can help make it stop.
So much *unable*, more can't *determine*. Like if *he got up.*

Actually, that I'm pretty clear on. Also that we stopped
the guy trying to shoot our buddies down. That guy got shot.
Rocket Man had it coming. The old man did not.
I was unable to determine whether or not he got up.

Twelve-Hour Shifts

A drone pilot works a twelve-hour shift, then goes home
to real life. Showers, eats supper, plays video games.
Twelve hours later he comes back, high fives, takes over the drone

from other pilots, who watch *Homeland*, do dishes, hope they don't
dream in all screens, bad kills, all slo-mo freeze-frame.
A drone pilot works a twelve-hour shift, then goes home.

A small room, a pilot's chair, the mic and headphones
crowd his mind, take him somewhere else. Another day
another dollar: hover and shift, twelve hours over strangers' homes.

Stop by the store, its Muzak, pick up the Cheerios,
get to the gym if you're lucky. Get back to your babies, play
Barbies, play blocks. Twelve hours later, come back. Take over the drone.

Smell of burned coffee in the lounge, the shifting kill zone.
Last-minute *abort mission*, and the major who forgets your name.
A drone pilot works a twelve-hour shift, then goes home.

It's done in our names, but we don't have to know. Our own
lives, shifts, hours, bounced off screens all day.
A drone pilot works a twelve-hour shift, then goes home;
fresh from twelve hours off, another comes in, takes over our drone.

Easy to Lie

They *get their diggers up*, they say
of people ostentatious in their dignity.

Streets ahead, they say of bright
children, and how it's *easy to lie*

on another man's wounds. They talk like this,
my people. My people not just the Irish

but anybody who'll admit
how cruel human cruelty can get.

BigDog

Tenderness for one machine, this one, but not
another. I love my car because it's mine, a Dodge
Charger because it's hot. The cartoony, childlike,
bulbous blind head of the Predator, the implicit
promise it'll save our soldiers' lives, make me love it.
I love the angles of black helicopters, stealth
Blackbirds, the facets on their bodies like they're
gems. I have a pewter magnet of a Blackbird,
want a plush child's toy of a Predator drone.

I love Zambonis and Jersey barrier movers, the way
they smooth and order, liquid, straighten, shift.
Concrete Jersey barriers slip in one side and out
the other like teeth in a zipper, salt water taffy, rope.

A man kicks BigDog in the video, shoves
it over. He makes it stumble, retreat, regain
its balance. *Come on, BigDog! You can do it,*
BigDog! BigDog is a robot. It can carry
heavy things for you. It wants to help,
if want is what it's made for. What we're
made for: wanting more. BigDog looks
like two ninjas carrying a heavy box. One ninja
walking backwards, both lifting their feet
too high. Like I walked home when I got high
with the waitresses after dishwashing shifts.
The Hobart: another machine I loved. I'd walk
like that, high-stepping, trying to make it home
without a scratch. Is that the tenderness?
The BigDog looks afraid, cautious? Adolescent,
high? BigDog has no face. BigDog can't see
where we're going. He only needs to know what we
need carried. He only wants to carry more for us.

LOFTY VIEW

Perhaps I could have been mistaken for bin Laden, too.
—John Sifton, "A Brief History of Drones," *The Nation*

Our young people fly our drones surrounded by high-tech TVs.
We're like rich villains in James Bond movies:

petting our Persians, watching our victims on screens. A drone
first fired a Hellfire missile in '01. We called the infrared *Kosovo*,

the missile *tank-killer*: it was *just beautiful*. Beautiful
before, before we knew what to hit. '02, we killed

a guy who was tall like bin Laden, John
Sifton, Abe Lincoln, my father. Daraz Khan,

a farmer, was tall, so now he's dead. You can set
a Hellfire missile and forget it. It goes on its own, gets

what it wants. A dog we trained to take out your throat.
We're flying killer robot planes: this instant, they're out

there, for us. And here: the Predator drone that made
that first mistake is up, displayed in D.C.'s Air and Space

Museum. It's kind of sweet that we're so sure
we're never really wrong. But drones crash, or

we lose them, or we think we see the bad guys
and hit a wedding, a funeral, two kids on a bike.

Heirloom

The *New York Times* reveals a man has bought,
at auction, a forty-five-hundred-dollar mummified
hand. *Hopefully it doesn't have any bad*
seeds attached, he said, the sort of line
that should be followed with "he quipped." We know
what he almost means: a curse, a vengeful mummy,
his rest disturbed, his corpse exhumed, his hand—
long ivory nails, frayed linen, delicate bones
in a tannic sort-of leather—broken off,
and sold at auction. The hand-buyer intends
it as an heirloom for his kids. Across
the country, warm toast in our mouths, we shake
our heads, turn to our spouses, smack the paper and say
It's a goddamn mummy's hand, you stupid fuck,
as if the hand bestowed its owner with
the power to hear collective common sense.
The Monkey's Paw, The Hand of Glory, now in New York
it drums its fingers, biding its endless time.

Law of Torment

After Jill Lepore

When *military law would not apply.*
Nor would the laws of war. Eye for an eye,

instead. Or more. Two eyes? Twenty for
one? *Lawful captives taken in Just Warres,*

we called enslaved Algonquians back in the day,
like that's legit. We show up. Okay. Straight off we violate

Habeas Corpus, *the law of nations, the rule*
of law over war. Our exceptionalism means we, too,

can kill innocents, or citizens, like Al Queda when
a *gleaming skyscraper became a tomb.* We went

a little crazy with the torture techniques: the waterboard, *Fear*
Up Harsh and *We Know All*, stuff we picked up from SERE. SERE:

the training we gave our good guys
on withstanding anti-law-of-nations types

in Russian Korea. Commies. Bad guys, what they do
to force a false confession out of you.

Big Data Overlords

The *Times* tells us about bimbots, chatbots, spambots; they *piece
together phrases that seem relevant.* I like this. I read it to Josey, add

Like anybody, right? She nods, distracted, says *You want coffee?* Yes.
Not relevant, Josey: well-played. But any human sleepy, startled, is just

piecing it together, a day at a time, call and response. Robotic: *More
snow, huh? Hang in there, man. See ya! Livin' the dream.* Now robots sleep

and wake like we do, shut down when we would, were we that smart.
Spambots never drunk-text, write pissed emails to the boss. They go

radio-silent, fool the breathing us. We the people, the weak, the ones
with bodies, all this blood. My father joined Twitter, the interwebs tell me,

but how can I tell it's really him? I text him, message my mom. Dad's
on Facebook, mom's in airplane mode. *Earth to Jill* she used to yell

over the TV, turned up to be louder than her. More than half of all tweeters
are bots, the *Times* blah-blah-blahs on my phone. E-cigarettes glow red

and blue in bars: delicious. Our robot overlords aren't coming for us;
they have already come. We have met the enemy, and they're

darn useful. Running our lives through the iCal, directing our gaze
on the train. I'm ready for you, robots, want more metadata, please.

The imaginot line, Susan calls the stripe marking first downs on TV
football fields; I want one marking my progress crosstown. And Rich's

afterlife—*one big database: all the broken glasses, sneezes, kisses, etc.*
All the answered emails, caught glances. Coffees, lost socks, held hands.

Reaper

Reaper. Just following orders, still death
personified. *The end of the world, and the reapers
are angels.* The Lord is my shepherd; my
shepherd, my reaper, I shall I shall not
want. Reaper all-seeing, untired, unbored.

The whip-smart Jesus in Matthew
Thirteen? He's parable-crazy. He makes them up, breaks
them down: *Gather together first the tares,
and bind them in bundles to burn them.* Good
seeds and bad, complicated harvest coming up.

Who hath ears to hear, let him hear
these metaphors, terrible parables, free for picking up
off the ground. The ground around Trinity,
the atomic test site? Still hot. *Break,
blow, burn.* We breathed sand in, rained it down

in Geiger-dazzling beauty, a sea-foam green
surprise. American ingenuity, foresight, imagination.
*For whosoever hath, to him shall be given, and he
shall have abundance: but whosoever hath not, from him
shall be taken away even that which he hath.*

I Dream We Try Gun

I dream we try gun manufacturers as terrorists
and win. The Gun Industry's a team of sneering
white guys. Suits, saying all the wrong stuff. Am I
a lawyer? Witness? I am Julia Roberts in *Pelican Brief*
and *Erin Brockovich*. I say crossfire more than terrorism,
and schoolkids, every day. Their lawyer's smarmy,
dismissive, saying *Sandy Hook* and *of course
those beautiful children* and I say No, the other ones.
The ones you make us take for granted, the ones
that you can't see. Black kids shot dead daily, whole
zones we've given up. He smirks. *What about cars, cars
kill people.* Says *bears, terrorists, sharks.* But in the dream
I'd said enough. Whatever I said worked. Everyone laughed
at the gun guys, gun guys crying *shark.* We won, won
instant reparations. Our dead spun back to before.
Not like zombies, not like the monkey's paw. Just
back, all better, all gun deaths now undone. Dried blood
gone bright, pulling back into her pink slacks, his black
hoodie's holes, now healed. At first we're scared; it's not
just kids, it's everyone. Good guys and bad, soldiers
from forever now come home. We get them all back. To help
with what's next. And we know who the terrorists are.

Try

You just try to hand them some hot chocolate,
said EMTs at the scene, of the unscathed
milling in shock, after someone opened fire.

Looking at Saints and Talking about Robots

Susan and I look at Saints at the Met, track
down Lucy, Catherine, Justina, palm
branches and swords, peaceful told-you-so
expressions. We walk out past *Cornus mas*
and daffodils, forsythia, to the Frick. Past
a woman, her iPhone, her yelling out *FRICK*.
The FRICK MUSEUM. We snicker. Frick
and Clark, the fricken Met. At the Frick
we see a flock of Piero della Francescas. Angels
with blue or pink or ochre wings around
a sturdy Mary, trying to keep the baby from
that rose. All day we've talked about robots;
scary-sexy ones in *Metropolis*, *Stepford Wives*,
how now we're not turned on, just terrified.
The boys at Boston Dynamics love headlines
saying BigDog's creepy, pieces freaking out about
SquishBot. Why now are we afraid? I think it's
Terminator, blame that guy for everything. But
Susan's smart, blames The Industrial Revolution,
The Big IR, how everybody lost their jobs. We also
lost our limbs, then, early on. John Henry, steam.
Do we want to die with our hammer in our hand?
I guess we sort of do. We love our iPhones,
love our cars, but we've decided we're the ones
who get a face, who get to win, who get a say.

John Clare's First Trip to London

When they saw anything out of the ordinary Clare would murmur
"Oh Christ."
    —Jonathan Bate, *John Clare*

The London Mail overturned *Oh Christ* an anthem
sung by the children of St. Martin-in-the-Fields

Oh Christ a thirteen-year-old girl whispering
as many gentlemen as pleased would be admitted

Oh Christ the Birmingham theatre burned, the fine first-class ship
THE LADY BANKS—*Oh Christ*—bound for Calcutta *Oh Christ*

Mr. Edward Grainger's lectures on anatomy in his rooms
Oh Christ miserable objects starving and freezing—*Oh Christ*—

in all the public places—*Oh Christ*—
Oh Christ Oh Christ Oh Christ

Big Stink, Necessary Evil

We named the plane that followed
the *Enola Gay* to Hiroshima *Necessary
Evil*. *Big Stink* followed the Nagasaki
one, *Bockscar*. *Big Stink, Necessary Evil*
took the photos you know from when
we bombed Japan. Google for them
and you see the plane itself, Our
Lady of the Nose Cone: blonde,
badly drawn, be-bikinied pre-Bikini
Atoll. She straddles a smoking cityscape
mapped out on a Japanese flag. *Enola Gay*
didn't get a lady, a sketch of ruin; just
a name. Photos of Fat Man and Little Boy,
deployed: black and whites of mushroom clouds
ringed and haloed, expanding quick across
horizons from 30,000 feet. Fresh cartographic
perspective. Mountains in the distance fade
and blur like in a painting. The cloud is puffy,
dense. Ring crisp and lovely in detail. It rises twice
as high as the planes, blots out that landscape, lost
in real time. Rips a billowed tear in this new map.

Code Names

ABOVE BOARD. CLEAR QUEST.
ABLE ALLY, ALLIED ACTION.
JUST CAUSE. EVEN STEVENS.

BRAVE HERO, EAGLE SCOUT, CLEAN HUNTER.
PROJECT GRACE.
NOBLE EAGLE; CREDIBLE DOVE.

CLUSTER FORTUNE, BONUS DEAL, GLORY TRIP.
FAT CAT, GANGSTER, PRIVATEER. FAST TALK.

CRAZY HAWK, TWISTEDPATH.
GRISLY HUNTER. DULL KNIFE.

EPIC FURY.

HEART ACHE.

FACE IT.

Mars

It is a place with a past but without a history.
—Robert Crossley, *Imagining Mars: A Literary History*

A blank slate. A red blank slate and what
did we go and do? Canaled it. Imagined it
canaled. Blank slate, red, we filled
with little green men, with fighting machines.
Here where we have trod, trod, trod, our little
minds too bleared and seared, too psyched
about Suez, the Panama. Everything looks
like a hammer to a nail. No, wait: like a nail.
If you're a hammer. We imagined not just people
like us but better ones, faster. Couldn't see
the nothing for the trees. Named our made-up
not-there canals all things like Cyclops, Daemon.
Made up things like Hades. Things like Styx.

Bad Decisions

I'm not hungry. I'm wearing
these shoes. I'll have

another drink. Here's
my credit card. I'm

not wearing a bra. I'm
not brushing my hair. I

am going to be a poet. I am going
down this slide.

The Beautiful Woman

The beautiful woman opposite me on the bus is laughing
and fat. I love her braided hair. I want her ring, her laughing
mouth. I love her so much I take her picture. She is on the phone.
I think she knows I'm taking her picture. I think she doesn't care.
I love her spill of thigh-fat freed from that rise of grey knit skirt.
She doesn't care we're trying not to stare.We only wish
whoever she's teasing on the phone was us. *No, no, no!* She
can barely get it out, says something in a laugh-choked
half-bus-drowned patois. She makes me want to pack the pounds
on both my thighs, go back to the time I found frosted blue eyeliner
like hers. I was twelve, didn't know the hundred ways happiness felt.
It's always like this for her: she moves through a world that's wilting
with love. All the world's busses filled with dopey smilers, every
face on every sidewalk beaming back at her, wishing her well.

Devil Pod

For Gail Mazur

My devil pod poem will not be better than yours.
You can talk about how they punctured tires

in WWII.
Mine will have you

in it, and us laughing. It will have internet
research! Quote, *could also be called BAT NUT,*

unquote. My sources have names like *luckymojo.com.*
I'll start with you giving me the pods

after I gave you whatever: chicken pie? I'll go on
to say how lunch is a killer. No, an assassin!

If you break up your day and have lunch with a friend,
BAM, you will never write anything ever again.

When it was time to hug goodbye, I
said *Let's both write*

poems about the devil pods. I held on when you stiffened.
I whispered *Mine will be better.* So you'd laugh. Now it's written.

My First Murderer

Though our lives—
    First Murderer, *Macbeth* III.1.140

Nobody cares about the murderers or
their lives. They didn't even have names.
We are men, they say. And then defend
their falls with familiar excuses, mitigating
circumstance. *The vile blows and buffets of
the world incensed* one, made him *reckless
to spite the world.* The other—my first
murderer—*so weary with disasters* he'd do
anything *to mend it.* Teaching *Macbeth* in the prison,
I have the men write speeches for the unnamed,
numbered murderers, give them the voices Macbeth
couldn't hear. I say I think they're more human
than Macbeth is, talk about empathy, ambition,
desire. They're so afraid of the *thees* and *thous*,
always say *Shakespeare* with fear, can't hear
what's happening until they put words in their
murderers' mouths, show them to be human, scared
of nothing, willing to try whatever works.

Calling Predator "I"

After Lt. Col. Matt J. Martin, *Predator: The Remote-Control
Air War over Iraq and Afghanistan: A Pilot's Story*

My job was mostly to circle and stare and wait:
hover over my shift, then high five the other guy.
I called Predator *I*—I was here, and thousands of miles away.

Sometimes my shift would end but I'd want to stay
on. See it through. Keep the bad guys in my sights.
Just sit tight, circle and stare and wait

while the next pilot hung out, watched, cheered me on. I'd say
what I saw to the analysts, wait to hear I was right.
I already called Predator *I*—thousands of miles away

I'd be banking, turning. Or just still, still there. I'd stay
on the spot; watch, report, unseen hours of their time.
I could continue to circle and stare and wait

all night, all day; all my shift, anyway.
I'd forget where I really was, how, which chunk of time.
I already called Predator *I*; thousands of miles away

I paid more attention than I could at home, my day
off. If anybody asked how I was, I'd just say *fine*.
But in my mind I'd still be circling, staring, waiting,
calling Predator *I*, thousands of miles away.

Armed

After Lt. Col. Matt J. Martin, *Predator: The Remote-Control
Air War over Iraq and Afghanistan: A Pilot's Story*

Sometimes I felt like God: thunderbolts from afar.
Predator could watch the same spot all day.
I was a patient, silent hunter. I was armed.

Those guys never saw what hit them; you can't get far
after Hellfire's launched. You can run, maybe pray.
Sometimes I felt like God: thunderbolts from afar.

When we hit? The screens go white. The house or car
or whatever pretty much just goes away.
I was a patient, silent hunter. I was armed.

I saw bodies, severed limbs. Once, just parts
of the horse the guy rode in on. There were good days—
sometimes I felt like God: thunderbolts from afar—

taking out some asshole when he starts
burying an IED ahead of a convoy, do what it takes
for our guys on the ground. Stay *patient, silent, armed.*

You see some fucked up shit. That's the war—
you get used to it. You watch and you wait.
Sometimes I felt like God: thunderbolts from afar.
I was a patient, silent hunter. I was armed.

50

Still Death

An unfortunate byproduct of waging this kind of war.
—Lt. Col. Matt J. Martin, *Predator: The Remote-Control Air War
over Iraq and Afghanistan: A Pilot's Story*

On the screen or on the ground, death observed is still death.
Sparkle a target, fire a Special K, hope nobody moves. Then it hits
a bicycle. One boy pedaling, one on the handlebars—broken, bent—

it wasn't there twenty-three seconds ago. It was insurgents,
a whole truckload. We double-checked, declared a clear target.
On the screen or up close and dusty, death observed is still death.

Every bomb's a strategic failure, even if it's a tactical success
I heard an F-16 commander say once: That fits with this,
two little bodies on the screen. Flung from their bicycle, broken and bent.

We saw bad guys burying mortar tubes, fired, held our breath
till a bright flash washed out the screen: direct hit.
Bad guys are easier to watch die. But death is still death,

and we're the ones killing. It's not just *death observed* I meant:
I started calling the Predator *I*—I hover, I watch—two weeks in,
so *I* knocked two boys from a bike, saw it broken and bent.

Or, sure, bad guys, probably just locals looking to make rent,
get paid to pop off a round. Do they count as jihadists?
On the screen or on the ground, a death observed is still death.
I'm not forgetting the bicycle, two boys. Broken and bent.

Of a Piece

Our ears are tuned to scraping
desks in rows. Chalk on a chalkboard,

a bell at noon. So our eyes
rise, follow the chalk, what's left behind.

A piece of chalk, dust like pixels,
pressing silk to slate. Each seat facing

the erasing. Looking for what's left, the rest.
Wanting to know what'll be on the test.

In The Next Chapter

In the next chapter, we consider the strengths of autonomous battlefield weaponry in contrast to the shortcomings of human warfighters.
—Ronald C. Arkin, *Governing Lethal Behavior in Autonomous Robots*

Next chapter it's
all over. Next just *we*
give up. The micro apiary
drones around us, sounds
like nothing much. Just
shifting air, the hair
on the back of your neck
knowing more than
you do. It's everywhere—
before, behind, between,
above, below—we've given up,
O my America, everything, all
the little human perks. What we first
heard low, calm, saying
sounds like you'd like to speak
to a representative says, still
calm, *now put your hands up.*

Rat's Ass

A rat's ass, a flying
fuck, shit, damn,
crap—what we wouldn't
give: a hoot,
a tinker's damn.
Who ever has believed
anyone who said it?
We lowball it. We
kick the ground.
Not one of us really
means it, means
what we think we
wish we mean. We do give
a rat's ass, a flying fuck, two
shits; the urgency, profanity
transparent as rain.
I don't give a rat's ass.
Do what you want.
Angry, or hurt and lonely.
Here trembling, this one
close to tears. *I don't*
give a flying
fuck, they lie, giving it
all away.

The Money

After Julie Mehretu's *Mural*

I went to visit the money. Which is a mural
at Goldman Sachs which don't even
get me started. They don't let you any
closer than the sidelines, security desk
on the right. No way past the uniformed
men, electronic gates, but, *ma'am*,
you can exit the building, look in
through rain-spotted plate glass. I got
ma'am-ed, smiled, stood in the rain outside
the money. Here's who I saw go in, who I saw
belongs there, who it has to be said never even
glanced at the money: short white men in natty
suits—is it rude to note they're short? If I admit
the suits are natty? A beautiful woman
in red-soled shoes. The red-soled shoes brown
suede. Red soles mean, yes, they are money.
Another woman with her laptop in a cush
grey flannel felt case. Money. Classy, classy
money. These people know how to shop. These people
are nice and dry. I'm wet, in a wet
blue raincoat, fogging up a nose-height spot
on the window. Hands, forehead pressed like a child's
to the shark tank, looking in at the beautiful
money. It looks like this: confusion
of streamlined detail, all the colors. Calders
in a blender. Flight paths, grids over maps over
wires. Plus an orange square I really like. More
than you can see at one time with just
your eyes. You have to pace back and forth
in the rain, get glimpses of money. Between
columns. Through the rain-spotted glass.

Times Square

Sailors in uniform, bristled hair imagining
ticker tape flicking over these screens. Drag queens

speak Spanish, gather on the island, lean back
on their kitten heels. The ground they walk on

is here clay tile, here concrete—different ages,
seams, aggregates revealed. Through the grate,

foil wrappers glint in a litter of butts. Tourists with cockney accents ask
the man selling *Cheney/Satan '08* stickers where's the Ruby Tuesday's.

Ruby Tuesday's? He looks around, aggrieved. He doesn't know.
In the shadow of the Booth, the Schoenfeld,

the Jacobs and Golden, he's telling everyone
Wolf Blitzer doesn't have the balls.

Taxis and limos in their Times Square shuffles, *SUBWAY*
in lights, neon NYPD. A red rover line of pedestrians

looks right in unison, jaywalks in unison.
Doppler of skateboards, yellowcabs, horns. Mica

in the sidewalk, pixels against the sky. A plaque lists
the city's Medal of Honor recipients, Civil War

through Vietnam. Private Bart, Coxswain Betham,
Trumpeter Keenan, Major Lee and the others under

Army, Navy, Airforce, Marines seals the exact size
of manhole covers. A little girl in a fur hat runs

to her father, who is wearing a fur hat. He calls to her
in French. He's filming the whole thing.

Imperial War Museum, Duxford

I ask to see the early drone and the docent's
startled, confused. Drones lacking
the glamour of B-52s, the supersonic
Concorde. The wooden-propellered Falconer
is sleek as canoe, red as a wagon. The kind
Marilyn Monroe built: it's in the pictures
of her as a child bride, a Rosie-the-Riveter
type. A baby is crying, a boy with Tourette's
swears. All through the museum you
see names, see what names can do.
Strikemaster, Liberator, Vampire.
Hellcat, Avenger. Victor, Hind. *Calling
All Everyone! Calling All Everyone*!
shouts the boy through the playground's megaphone.
Calling All Everyone! he's shouting again,
from the top of a fake control tower.

Brandon Bryant: MQ-1 Predator Sensor Operator

He lives in Montana now. Talks to Canadian radio shows,
German magazines. He coaches wrestling, still has to tell us

everything. How it works, how many screens. How many fly
one drone. *Fourteen*, and *two*. He marks targets, the other guy

sends the Hellfire. *The room is dark*, he saw too much, wished
his *eyes would rot*. He tried to talk, got hushed,

got told *to just shut up and color.* He says *We saw an eye*.
What's an eye? Bad guys *light a tire on fire,*

soften the blacktop, bury a bomb. *And the cool
metal, hot asphalt would make sort of an eye.* "Was it clear to you

*that there was a loss of life?
How many people died*

that day, Brandon? What was that like for you?" So I hate
the Canadian radio host, but he's the only way

to hear this. Streaming, next to "Saskatchewan Weekend,"
next to "Canada Reads." *Five* and *I never wanted to see that happen again.*

To see that happen, or this: *Around the building a small human body runs
around the corner to where the front*

*of the building to where the door was. The missile
connects and the building collapses, crumbles, and there's nothing, no little*

*body. I look at the pilot and asked, Was that a person, was that
a kid? And he's like, Yeah, I think it was. And we asked, we have this chat*

*program that we can communicate with other entities that are involved
and we asked and the person was like, No, it was a dog. It was a dog.*

Stoning the Drone

The MQ-1 Predator carries the Multi-spectral
Targeting System: electro-optical, infrared.
Laser designator, illuminator.
It can see and hit its target from miles away.
The Air Force and the CIA both use them,
but no one's claimed the one brought down last week.
An RPG? An error? Something took
five million dollars' worth of our tech down
so you can see, on YouTube, Afghans gathered
around it, laughing, throwing stones. The young
guy filming circles children, shows some men
approach, but not too close. Then, seconds in,
you start to hear the thunk of rock against
the hull, which makes him laugh: *Oh, ho!* The way
we joke *Oh HO, my friend. Ho, SHIT. GodDAMN.*
The only word I understand is *drone*.
Our cameraman laughs, amazed—the witch is dead!
Now everybody's throwing stones. Dust rises
up from kids' missed throws: we hear their Pashto
*dag!*s. Cameraman shows the stony ground; his
glitchy shadow staggers around. His happiness
contagious, his point of view so clear. His friend,
a grinning older man, reaches, takes the camera,
gets him in the frame. For a moment all we see
is hands, their lined palms, then bright light of lens
turned clumsily to sun. Then there's our guy,
beside the drone he's caught on film. Posing, proud,
like every kid by every science project.
They're throwing rocks as if it's over now, as if
they got The One True Drone, as if it hurts us back.

Bin Laden's Burial and the Bureau of Investigative Journalism

AP tells us no sailors watched,
traditional Islamic procedures
were followed. Someone praying
barefoot *Allahu Akbar*, O Lord forgive
this dead body. A man washing his body
with camphor water, then again with plain.
Bin Laden, the bad guy, washed clean. Wrapped
in a white sheet, placed in a weighted bag.
People lifted the board with his body, tipped
it so he slid to the sea. That month our Reapers
reduced one moving car in Doga Mada Khel
to ashes. We seem to mostly kill the ones
we mean to kill. We killed bin Laden—*Obama
got Osama!*—but our last drone strike
before bin Laden died, killed 25:
20 militants, 2 women, 3 children.
A 12-year-old, Atif.

said the guy the news asked when Iran
got our RQ-170 Sentinel. It's a high-altitude
spy plane. It's the new U-2, the spy plane
we used since the fifties. The U-2 looks
like the fifties; the Sentinel looks like the future.
Beautiful, batwing: paper airplane, *papier-mâché,*
something you can buy in an Apple store,
something you could put in your mouth.
We lost it. Now it's in a school gym in Iran,
school gyms being tricky to bomb.
With stars-and-stripes banners, blue field
of stars replaced with skulls, slogans crossing
the stripes: *The US Can't Mess With Us* and
We'll Crush America Underfoot. We're messing
with them. They're under
our foot. The Sentinel's nicknamed
The Beast of Kandahar although
it's lovely, and doesn't have guns.
Just looking. With its soft white curves,
one-eyed Storm Trooper face. When we lost
a U-2 in Russia the pilot bailed out,
didn't cyanide himself, though some people
thought that he should. Now
the end-of-the-world guy on *Air Force News*
shakes his head, surprised our pretty
new drone didn't just self-destruct:
Is the world really that poorly run?

New Year's Ghazal, after Ghalib

2014, you are All-You-Can-Eat glamour. The poetry pours out
of bars, sparkling streets. Lord, keep it up: pearls before movie stars

at dusk, midnight, almost light. What? We're having the best time, talking
Black Ops, Café Sushi, robots, End Times. Fall of Rome, atomic theory, stars

in Dickinson, in Keats. A brick from the Ziggurat of Ur, a face from Trajan's
column. I don't have to get it to love it, love us: the very soil, heavy stars

and metals, black holes, your science book, his grapevine. How can we help
  carry
what-all our friends are bearing? Their griefs, their hungers, unlucky stars.

We're busy with baloney, borrowed trouble. Only asleep do we know
there's blood on our hands. When we wake up, the unsteady stars

are spy-drones, satellites. We wish we may, we wish we might stay safe
and warm, blacked out with our big brother, under the angry stars.

War Alphabet

Alphabet de la Guerre is a picture book from Brussels, *Pour
les Grands et les Petits*. No date, just WWI. We still think this
is what war is: canteens, broad shoulders, helmets
shining. Boots, so much barbed wire. A is for Aviation. B,
Barbelés, scene of concertina wire. C is for Canon; D, *Drapeau*.
The pictured men are carved from wood. Tired, hulking, hefting
shells, kissing the red fringe of a flag. E: Elisabeth, a sister
of mercy, tenderly tending a jaundiced bandaged man. G
for *Grenadiers*, a helmeted soldier lobbing one toward
red flames, smoke, a barricade. H is for *Héros*: one
grim man handing a medal to another. Pink cheeks, half
blinded by bandage, his mouth too uncertain to be O.
Incendie: a line of refugee faces, babies, hands crowding
the frame from a ruined village, flickers of smoke, of flame.
L: *Lance-Flammes*, a gas-masked figure's new
flamethrower, boxy and mean. The freshest tech they had
then, out there shooting, saving lives. We still recognize Tank,
Union, Waggonet full of shells. But now we're all alphabet:
NSA, CIA, V for the failed VA. P is for Private Contractors,
for Predator, B for Black Ops, Black Sites. G for Guantanamo,
A for Abu Ghraib, R for Ravens, for Reapers, our remote
control avatars, hovering far from our American home.

RECENT TITLES FROM ALICE JAMES BOOKS

Madwoman, Shara McCallum
Contradictions in the Design, Matthew Olzmann
House of Water, Matthew Nienow
World of Made and Unmade, Jane Mead
Driving without a License, Janine Joseph
The Big Book of Exit Strategies, Jamaal May
play dead, francine j. harris
Thief in the Interior, Phillip B. Williams
Second Empire, Richie Hofmann
Drought-Adapted Vine, Donald Revell
Refuge/es, Michael Broek
O'Nights, Cecily Parks
Yearling, Lo Kwa Mei-en
Sand Opera, Philip Metres
Devil, Dear, Mary Ann McFadden
Eros Is More, Juan Antonio González Iglesias, Translated by Curtis Bauer
Mad Honey Symposium, Sally Wen Mao
Split, Cathy Linh Che
Money Money Money | Water Water Water, Jane Mead
Orphan, Jan Heller Levi
Hum, Jamaal May
Viral, Suzanne Parker
We Come Elemental, Tamiko Beyer
Obscenely Yours, Angelo Nikolopoulos
Mezzanines, Matthew Olzmann
Lit from Inside: 40 Years of Poetry from Alice James Books, Edited by Anne
    Marie Macari and Carey Salerno
Black Crow Dress, Roxane Beth Johnson
Dark Elderberry Branch: Poems of Marina Tsvetaeva, A Reading by Ilya
    Kaminsky and Jean Valentine
Tantivy, Donald Revell
Murder Ballad, Jane Springer
Sudden Dog, Matthew Pennock
Western Practice, Stephen Motika
me and Nina, Monica A. Hand

Alice James Books has been publishing poetry since 1973. The press was founded in Boston, Massachusetts as a cooperative wherein authors performed the day-to-day undertakings of the press. This collaborative element remains viable even today, as authors who publish with the press are also invited to become members of the editorial board and participate in editorial decisions at the press. The editorial board selects manuscripts for publication via the press's annual, national competition, the Alice James Award. Alice James Books seeks to support women writers and was named for Alice James, sister to William and Henry, whose extraordinary gift for writing went unrecognized during her lifetime.

Designed by Mike Burton
Printed by McNaughton & Gunn